LUQMAN - THE WISE MAN WITH ROOTS IN AFRICA, WHO IS RELATED TO ALL MANKIND

Shakir Maris Abdullah
Luqman - The Wise Man With Roots In Africa, Who Is Related To All Mankind

Published by Spines
ISBN: 979-8-89691-095-4

LUQMAN - THE WISE MAN WITH ROOTS IN AFRICA, WHO IS RELATED TO ALL MANKIND

A MUST READ FOR ALL SEEKERS OF PROGRESS

SHAKIR MARIS ABDULLAH

DEDICATION

To those who seek truth, progress, and deeper understanding: This book of Luqman's African roots will excite and titillate your curiosity, guiding you to seek more truth, find more truth, and live more truth.

CONTENTS

Foreword ix
Acknowledgments xi
Introduction xiii
Reminder xv

1. PART ONE 1
2. Message From the Author 17
3. PART TWO 19
4. Message From the Author 27
5. PART THREE 29

Conclusion 37
Bibliography 41
Epilogue I 43
Epilogue II 47

FOREWORD

This book is perhaps the first of its kind that points directly to the pure ancestry of Africans' mannerisms. This work reconnects Africans who live in different countries with a historical African figure of great personage. Luqman's reverence and veneration are beyond question and of great importance to Africans and all other people. Luqman had been only a cloaked silhouette in the annals of history before the elucidation of his character in the Qur'an.

This book offers, without doubt, enrichments and visionary aims for the African intelligentsia. It is truly a remarkable disclosure of a previously dead record of advanced social progress that should be read by all African people dispersed throughout the world.

ACKNOWLEDGMENTS

As for the preparation of myself to undertake this task: All the praise belongs exclusively to the Almighty God, the Guardian, Evolver, Cherisher, and Sustainer of all the worlds.

I owe special thanks to any and all participants whose suggestions and input helped to redefine and perfect this work to reach the minds and hearts of the innocent, the ignorant, the deprived, the lost, the fortunate and unfortunate, and all believers.

INTRODUCTION

For centuries, African people have sought to elevate their status and dignity to a level of respect and appreciation. However, what they have sought, and continue to seek, has been very elusive because they had lost the fixed station of Divine Guidance through their ancestry. That status was established, solidified, and recognized through their "silent" ancestor, Luqman, the Wise Man of African descent.

One of the primary problems with African history is that its secrets were lost due to the forced diaspora or dispersion of Africans throughout the earth. The slave trade and the resulting resettlement or transplant of Africans caused them to suffer the greatest losses in their history, culture, and refinements. Therefore, the duly proportioned and balanced reunion of people of African descent is at a stalemate!

Yet, this humble work seeks to bring into sharp focus that which is of the greatest importance and was lost to the consciousness of African peoples. It is hoped that, through this work, that consciousness will re-emerge gradually and its fruits will be realized through our changing behavior for the better. The consciousness of divine guidance, which should be passed from parents to children or from generation to generation, brings into existence what Africans have sought to discover for centuries and will not disappoint them!

REMINDER

This book is not focused on or geared towards the current or past achievements of the African populace at all. Rather, it attempts to identify a legendary African mental attitude of high social standing that existed among one of their extinct ancestors.

This book will be comprised of three parts, subject to future additions. Part one is mainly concerned with the discovery and identification of this great African human being, whose discovery was truly serendipitous. Part two will observe and note the sagacity of this great African figure. Part three plays the role of an ombudsman to offset any conjecture of kinship perpetuation between Luqman and the Arabs that would destroy the innate ability to seek a just course.

The decision to divide this book into parts was made for the purpose of outlining different points in each part for reflection. Therefore, pay close attention to each sectional contour.

These sectional separations were also necessary so that readers may have time to think seriously about its contents for full and satisfactory appreciation, and to truly concentrate on the place (The Qur'an) where this vital information has been preserved and protected by Divine Authority all along.

All Praise Is Due To Allah!

PART ONE

It is not this work's interest to present an in-depth analysis of African history at this time but to acquaint the readers with a historical figure of excellence that needs to be recognized and explored for improved human development.

Despite the constant emphasis on African tragedies and mishaps suffered by Africans (of all residents, states, and countries) at the hands of others, many Africans (of all residents, states, and countries) have definitely inherited toxic behavior patterns that have altered their innate inclinations and proclivities to succeed in Allah's (God's) scene of things.

Once the psyche is modified to this magnitude and depth, it has to be renewed to its purpose and goal. Each person or individual is given the chance for development and progress toward the goal, which is Allah (God). However, the course or path pursued has to be accurate for the attainment of divine consciousness.

For Africans (of all residents, states, and countries), they have an ancestor who pursued such a course of accuracy that he was given the title "Luqman the Wise." The course or path he adhered to manifested divine consciousness to such a degree that it is unworthy for Africans (of all residents, states, and countries) to ignore this pattern of excellence.

This buried truth is the epitome of human achievement to its maximum and attempts to distinguish between Africans' mental attitude and social position with a former ancestor's mental attitude and social standing, whose achievements have been lost or completely forgotten altogether. In order to effect an accurate fact sheet, the text will commence and conclude with highly acceptable Qur'anic translators. This vehicle is necessary and appropriate to link this crucial reclamation.

"LUQMAN THE WISE"

Who is Luqman, and what have Qur'anic translators written about him?

S. Abul A'ala Maududi

Historically, Luqman is a disputed personage. In the dark centuries of ignorance, there was no compiled history.

The only source of information was the traditions that had been handed down for centuries. According to these, some people thought that Luqman belonged to the people of Ad and was a king of Yaman.

Relying on these traditions, Maulana Sayyid Suleman Nadui has expressed the opinion in *Ard al-Qur'an* that Luqman was a descendant of the believers who remained safe with the Prophet Hud after the destruction of the people of Ad by a divine torment. He was one of the kings of Yaman when it was ruled by the Ad. However, other traditions reported from some learned companions and their followers do not support this view.

Ibn Abbas says Luqman was a Negro slave, and the same is the opinion of Hadrat Abu Hurairah, Mujahid, Ikrimah, and Khalid ar-Rab'i. According to all of the following authors and translations provided, these pundits' commentaries have been taken from their translations and interpretations of *The Holy Qur'an.*

Hadrat Jabir bin 'Abdullah Ansari stated that he belonged to Nubah. Sa'id bin al-Musayyib says that he was an Egyptian Negro. These three sayings closely resemble one another. The Arabs generally called black people Negroes (Habashis) in those days, and Nubah is the country south of Egypt and north of Sudan. Therefore, calling the same person an Egyptian, a Nubian, and a Negro, despite the difference in words, is one and the same thing.

The elucidations made by Suhayli in *Raud al-Unuf* and Mas'udi in *Muruj adh-Dhahab* also throw some light on how the wisdom of this Sudanese slave spread in Arabia. They both agree that this person, though originally a Nubian, was an inhabitant of Madyan and Aylah (modern Aqabah). That is why he spoke Arabic, and his wisdom spread in Arabia.

Tafseer-e-Usmani

By: Allama Shabbir Ahmad Usmani

Vol. III, (pg. 1796)

Most scholars are of the opinion that Hazrat Luqman was not a prophet but a holy, pious man whom God had given wisdom, understanding, sobriety, and sagaciousness of a very high degree. Through wisdom, he opened those facts which are concordant with the teachings of the prophets. His wise admonitions and maxims have been proverbial in history.

Quoting a portion of his lessons and teachings in *The Holy Qur'an,* God, the Lord of Honour, has made him more eminent.

Note:

Opinions and research differ about the period and birthplace of Hazrat Luqman. Most of them say he was a Negro and lived in the age of David.

Translation And Commentary

By: T.B. Irving (pg. 226)

Among the Arabs, Luqman was a spiritual associate and possible grandnephew of the Old Testament prophet Job, similar to the fable-teller and wise man of Greece called Aesop. He is, in fact, the traditional Arab sage who fills much the same place in Arab folklore as Aesop (or the "Ethiopian") did among the Greeks.

The Meaning Of The Glorious Qur'an

By: Mohammed Marmaduke Pickthall (pg. 430)

Luqman takes its name from v.12 ff., which contains mention of the wisdom of Luqman, a sage whose memory the Arabs revered but who is unknown to Jewish Scripture. He is said to have been an African slave, and the fables associated with his name are so like those of Aesop that the usual identification seems justified.

Translation And Commentary

By: Ayatullah Agha H.M.M. Pooya Yazdi & S.V. Mir Ahmed Ali

Luqman is said to have been not an apostle of God but one blessed with an extraordinary or special endowment of wisdom. He was the nephew of Ayyub (Job) and had lived for a thousand years, from the time of David (Dawood) to the time of Jonah (Yunus). Once, when

Luqman was asleep, the angels called him, asking if he would like to be God's deputy on earth, to which he replied, saying that if that were the command of God, he would abide by it; but if God had asked about his desire or given him a choice, he would beg to be pardoned and spared from acting as such.

The angels asked why he said so, and he replied, saying that it was a great responsibility and a very difficult task to do justice among men, and he could not bear the burden. Some say that he was an Ethiopian carpenter whom the Greeks have called Aesop. He was a very obedient servant of the Lord and mostly remained silent, engrossed in higher thoughts.

Translation And Commentary

By: Maulana Muhammad Ali

The name of this chapter is taken from that of the sage to whose story it refers. Luqman was an Ethiopian, and his mention here testifies to the breadth of the fundamental principles of Islam alluded to in the last chapter.

Translation And Commentary

By: Abdullah Yusuf Ali

The sage Luqman, after whom this Sura is called, belongs to Arab tradition. Very little is known of his life. He is usually associated with a long life, and his title is Mu'ammar (the long-lived). He is referred by some to the age of the 'Ad people. He is the type of perfect wisdom. It is said that he belonged to a humble station in life, being a slave or carpenter, and that he refused worldly power and a kingdom.

Translation Of Vocabulary Of The Holy Qur'an

By: Dr. Abdullah Abbas Nadwi

'Luqman' was a sage. His wisdom is celebrated by Arabs. He was known even in the Jahiliyah period as a sage. Luqman is the name of two, if not three, persons famous in Arabian traditions. The first was of the family of 'Ad. The name of the second Luqman, called 'Luqman the sage,' occurs in the Qur'an.

According to Masudi, he was a Nubian freedman who lived in the time of David.

Translation and Commentary

By: Tafsir Ibn Kathir

Opinions:

The Salaf differed over the identity of Luqman. There are two opinions: was he a Prophet, or just a righteous servant of Allah without being a Prophet?

Sufyan Ath-Thawri said, narrating from Al-Ash'ath, from Ikrimah, from Ibn Abbas:

"Luqman was an Ethiopian slave who was a carpenter."

Abdullah bin Az-Zubayr said:

"I said to Jabir bin Abdullah: Did you hear about Luqman? He said: 'He was short with a flat nose and came from Nubia.'"

Yahya bin Sa'id Al-Ansari narrated from Sa'id bin Al-Musayyib that:

"Luqman was from the black peoples of (southern) Egypt and had thick lips. Allah gave him wisdom but withheld prophethood from him."

Al-Awza'i said:

"Abdur-Rahman bin Harmalah told me: A black man came to Sa'id bin Al-Musayyib to ask him a question, and Sa'id bin Al-Musayyib said to him: 'Do not be upset because you are black, for among the best of people were those who were black: Bilal, Mahja the freed slave of Umar bin Al-Khattab, and Luqman the Wise, who was a black Nubian with thick lips.'"

Translation and Commentary

By: Tafsir At-Tabari

Luqman was an Ethiopian slave who was a carpenter.

Therefore, Luqman is according to the following definitions:

S. Abul A'la Maududi	Negro Slave, Nubian, Egyptian Negro, Black People Negro, Sudanese Slave
Allama Shabbir Ahmad Usmani	Was Not A Prophet Negro, Holy Pious Man
T.B. Irving	Spiritual Associate, Sage
Mohammed Marmaduke Pickthall	Sage, African Slave
Ayatullah Agla H.M.M. Pooya Yazdi S.V. Mir Ahmed Ali	Not An Apostle Ethiopian, Ethiopian
Maulana Muhammad Ali	Ethiopian Sage
Abdullah Yusuf Ali	Slave, Carpenter
Dr. Abdullah Abbas Nadwi	Nubian Freedman
Tafsir Ibn Kathir	Ethiopian Slave, Carpenter, Nubian, Black People of Egypt, Not a Prophet
Tafsir At-Tabari	Ethiopian Slave, Carpenter
Abdul Mannan "Omar	A Non-Arab, Non-Israelite, African Prophet From Nubia

According to the collective opinions of these renowned scholars of the Qur'an, it appears that Luqman's origin is of African descent, despite the difference in words.

S. Abul A'la Maududi has provided in his widely accepted commentary regarding the use of different words: "Calling the same person an Egyptian, a Nubian, and a Negro, in spite of the difference in words, is one and the same thing." Applying this same logic to all the scholars' findings about Luqman—that he was a Negro slave, a Nubian, an Egyptian Negro, or a Sudanese slave, or an African, or an Ethiopian—are, in reality, one and the same thing.

As an additional reference, it must be mentioned that all these names are sobriquets to identify one kind or type of person or people. Moreover, Luqman's physical identity was of dark complexion, while his mental attitude was colorless. Visit part two for Luqman's true mentality. These explanations provide the answer to the previous question: Who was Luqman?

Additionally, there is one other area of Luqman's life that needs review for balance. According to the available commentary provided by scholars, Luqman was not a prophet or an apostle. Nor does the Qur'an indicate that Luqman was a prophet. This is very important to know so that people may not spend a lifetime seeking to achieve what was never intended! What is clear from both the Qur'an and the scholars is that Luqman was a holy, pious man, a spiritual associate, a man of unquestionable wisdom, and a sage.

Luqman opened through wisdom those facts which were concordant with the teachings of the Prophets. Therefore, Luqman's principles, precepts, and actions were contemporary with the principles, precepts, and actions of the Prophets.

It is this type of twin mentality that existed between Luqman and the Prophets that is absent from Africans' mentality and their better ancestor, Luqman the Wise's mentality. It is also necessary to mention at this time that it is a historical fact that Africans of all regions, states, and countries had to be acculturated to meet the labor-intensive plans prepared for them by their future slave owners. That transition accounts for one of the major setbacks in Africans' mental attitudes.

Nonetheless, Luqman was so obedient to divine guidance that he was made an emeritus for his adherence to divine principles and given a favorable position in the most honorable book in history for all times, *The Holy Qur'an.* Hence, the beginning of all wisdom is abiding by a divinely appointed system, or your progress—or attempted progress—will be abbreviated. This is the relationship Africans need to re-establish with God!

Luqman followed divine guidance, whereas most of today's guidance that is followed is mainly worldly or manly. Luqman was issued knowledge and judgment from a divine source, and he used both of these gifts in the service of Allah (God) to maintain the human structure prescribed by Allah through His divine messengers. For example, the admonitions that Luqman imparted to his son are ideally and basically what's missing from filial relationships among African American masculinity.

It is these types of admonitions that develop a precocious child into the ability to discriminate at early ages and make proper assessments during their adolescent and juvenile years. See David and Solomon's following example.

The sheep, on account of the negligence of the shepherd, got into a cultivated field (or vineyard) by night and ate up the young plants or their tender shoots, causing damage to the extent of perhaps a whole year's crop. David was king, and in his seat of judgment, he considered the matter so serious that he awarded the owner of the field the sheep themselves in compensation for his damage. His son Solomon, a mere boy of eleven, thought of a better decision, where the penalty would better fit the offense. The loss was the loss of the fruits or produce of the field or vineyard: the corpus of the property was not lost. Solomon's suggestion was that the owner of the field or vineyard should not take the sheep altogether but only detain them long enough to recoup his actual damage from the milk, wool, and possibly the young of the sheep, and then return the sheep to the shepherd. David's merit was that he accepted the suggestion, even though it came from a little boy. Solomon's merit was that he distinguished between corpus and income, and, though a boy, was not ashamed to put his case before his father. But in either case, it was Allah who inspired the true realization of justice.

So, we see from this narrative the growth that can emanate from children at early stages of their lives when they are divinely orientated. It would be wise to share Luqman's instructions with one's son or sons because wisdom seeks to solve difficulties and maintain structure, which is a combination of knowledge and understanding, as demonstrated in David and Solomon's adage. True wisdom is deontology and always didactic. Wisdom is so defined as such here because everything that the Divine teaches consists of these elements, and without them, there's nothing but the pursuit of passions, impulses, and desires.

One other point of interest: Luqman's instructions to his son are and were a longstanding establishment that has always been for the purpose of devolving the message of the Divine when divine contact hasn't been lost.

Qur'an 2:132

"And Abraham enjoined Upon his sons, And so did Jacob: "Oh, my sons! Allah hath chosen The Faith for you; then die not Except in the state of submission (to Me)."

Qur'an 2:133

"Were ye witnesses When Death appeared before Jacob? Behold, he said to his sons: "What will ye worship after me?" They said: "We shall worship Thy God and the God of thy fathers, Of Abraham, Ismail, and Isaac, The One (True) God; To Him do we submit."

Qur'an 11:42

"So the Ark sailed With them on waves (Towering) like mountains, And Noah called out To his son, who had Separated himself (from the rest): "O my son! Embark With us, and be not With the unbelievers!"

Qur'an 31:13

"Behold, Luqman said to his son, admonishing him: "O my son! Join not in worship (Others) with Allah: for False worship is indeed The highest wrongdoing."

This way of approaching one's son is not ahistoric, but rather a sound process toward implementing divine consciousness. This was the African's intended course or suggested course, as mirrored in Luqman's imagery at one point in time or another. If they don't seek to re-establish this intended or suggested course, they will always be derelict and remiss in their duties, responsibilities, and obligations, which, in reality, is really a punishment from God for abandoning divine guidance. The African populace, except for a small group, strikingly resemble the absence of what Luqman imparted to his son!

I am deeply cognizant and terribly affected by the transition that Africans have experienced and undergone. From lives of slavery to lives of plantation, from lives of plantation to lives of civil war, from lives of civil war to lives of so-called freedom, and the unforgettable and damaging effect it had and still has on their mental attitudes. Nevertheless, there are groups from the African global family that have surpassed that harsh movement and made considerable recovery. It is further suggested by the preceptory (Translators of The Qur'an) that

Luqman's memory was revered by the Arabs and that he was a holy, pious man whom God had given wisdom, understanding, sobriety, and sagaciousness of a very high degree. Also, it is reported that he was blessed with an extraordinary or special endowment of wisdom. Therefore, that recovery that some Africans of all residents, states, and countries have made and continue to make is really a fulfillment and continuation of human development from antiquity.

Then, there are other members from the African global family whose deportment assimilates the patterns specified earlier in this work that need guidance (Qur'an). The lessons provided in Luqman's narrative are the nexus to improving the human conscience for them (Africans) and all people in general. Part two will offer solutions to eliminate deviant and aberrant behaviors.

However, for the Africans, Maulana Muhammad Ali has put forth in his commentary that, "Luqman was an Ethiopian, and his mention testifies to the breadth of the fundamental principles of Islam." Therefore, this approach in retrospect for Africans is only a re-acquaintance of something once lost but now found, such as Faith, Charity, Enjoining The Right and Forbidding The Wrong, Prayers, and being patient in all challenges.

Therefore, Africans of all residents, states, and countries should seriously study and analyze Luqman's relationship with God and his son. Then, seriously study and analyze their overall relationship with God and their sons. Then compare the two. When these two evaluations are met, there evolves a clear picture of direction that requires acceptance, sincerity, and struggle to accomplish divine consciousness. If Luqman's lessons are allowed to officiate these types of relationships, then they would improve under the auspices of divine guidance. According to The Qur'an 33:40, there aren't going to be any more prophets, and the only thing left then is to fulfill the principles of human growth, which has really been the challenge for mankind.

Hence, Africans (of all residents, states, and countries) should commemorate their lost-found heritage by studying its particulars and familiarizing themselves with divine guidance (Qur'an), that they may be as wise as their progenitor, Luqman the Wise. This approach is extremely necessary so that the Qur'an may get the credit it truly deserves!

MESSAGE FROM THE AUTHOR

This effort has been an earnest attempt to familiarize Africans with a part of their history that is extant but has been overlaid by a variety of oversights and a lack of attention to salient suggestions surrounding Luqman's identity.

What this book has done is offer a step-by-step analogy of Luqman's origin and reconnect Africans with perhaps the most outstanding ancestor they could pay homage to.

Shakir Maris Abdullah

PART TWO

While the anomie of most Africans can be traced through many of the following known factors: lack of belief in the Divine, slavery, ignorance, illiteracy, broken homes, child neglect, drug and alcohol abuse, purloining, emotions, selfishness, arrogance, anger, asininity, violence, gambling, robbery, murder, malarkey, and a host of other factors which are not immune from consideration. These and other vices, however, modify a person's mental outlook and steal their healthy consciences.

This is what needs to be acknowledged and attended to for proper correction. All these factors, and many more, play a huge role in diminishing and destroying disciplines, principles, and moral accomplishments that a person may possess. Otherwise, the presence of these factors and vices will prevent disciplines, principles, and moral rectitude from being obtained and erected in your life.

Take, for instance, lack of belief in divine guidance. Lack of belief in divine guidance diminishes and destroys the wisdom that a person could receive from the divine message. However, this is not only true of lack of belief in divine guidance; it's also true of other vices and factors that diminish and destroy good virtues and values. Such as slavery: it diminishes and destroys family life, family values, and family traditions. Lying: it diminishes and destroys a person's truthfulness. Ignorance: it diminishes and destroys a person's awareness. Drug and alcohol addictions diminish and destroy a person's reasoning, intelligence, understanding, and conscience.

These analogies extend retroactively when applied to other vices.

This is exactly how people fall into states or conditions of oblivion, gradually substituting virtue for vice. This acclimation is perilous but can be obviated, as we shall see further on in this discourse, with the appropriate methods.

African Americans have been, and are, a people seeking to reconstruct principles and disciplines in their lives after slavery, which interrupted, diminished, and destroyed their family lives, their family values, their family traditions, and their family knowledge. As long as they continue to pursue this path of renovation, they will eventually be rewarded for their striving or given a new lease on life, so to speak. This transformation has actually occurred within many African American groups.

Additionally, one should now understand the birth of the African American tragedies, and all people's tragedies for that matter, from the aforementioned anomie, for it is truly a universal concept. Besides, the lessons of Luqman have offered the measures in which to repair such faulty aberrations.

Qur'an 31:12

"We bestowed (in the past) Wisdom on Luqman: 'Show (thy) gratitude to Allah.' Any who is (so) grateful Does so to the profit Of his own soul: but if Any is ungrateful, verily Allah is free of all wants, Worthy of all praise."

As mentioned earlier in Part One, true wisdom is deontology (ethics dealing with duty, moral obligation, and right action). This statement is true in more senses than one. If one looks to the command that Luqman executed ("Show (thy) gratitude to Allah"), one will find that this statement entails duty, moral obligation, and right action, which is carried out in the proceeding verses. We will also find, as we move forward, that these elements are inseparable from true wisdom.

In other words, duty, moral obligation, and right action *cannot* be apart from true wisdom. Whatever one is involved with—whether it's business, running a country, or teaching—these elements must be applied for constant human progress. One must constantly ask oneself, when engaged in activity, "Is this a duty? Is this a moral obligation? Or is this right action?" This is why governments continue to make amendments and changes to their laws and constitutions: because they lack this wisdom.

Qur'an 31:13

"Behold, Luqman said To his son admonishing him 'O my son! Join not in worship (Others) with Allah: for False worship is indeed The highest wrongdoing.'"

This is a duty, a moral obligation, and a hint to right action that one owes to one's son or sons. It preserves the maintenance of his ethics. When this has not been fulfilled, responsibility has not been performed.

The verb in Arabic for the word "said" is in perfect tense form, meaning a completed action. It's not until one completes this service that one has, in fact, made a prudent decision. Remember, it does not make a difference what level you are on or what your status quo may be; what is important is that you immediately begin to enact these lessons in a practical way.

Qur'an 31:14

"And We have enjoined on man (To be good) to his parents: In travail upon travail Did his mother bear him. And in years twain Was his weaning: (hear The Command), Show gratitude To Me and to thy parents: To Me is (thy final) Goal."

It's not an option to treat parents in a way other than how Allah has prescribed they should be treated. Allah has enjoined that a certain treatment be accorded to parents for the pain that the mother endured in childbirth and the weaning that followed thereafter to rear the child. This treatment of parents should be exemplified in loving and caring ways for their parental assistance. Gratitude should be equally accorded to Allah by fulfilling this function.

Qur'an 31:15

"But if they strive To make thee join In worship with Me Things of which thou hast No Knowledge, obey them not; Yet bear them company In this life with justice (And consideration), and follow The way of those who Turn to Me: In the End the return of you all is to me, And I will tell you All that ye did."

One thing that should definitely be emphasized here, which has never been expressed or brought forth before, is this: How can a child know when they are being asked to join in worship with Allah in things of which they have no knowledge? They can't, unless they are raised *only* under the guidance of Allah. This is one of the main reasons why the worship of personalities exists more than the worship of Allah in many instances.

When one looks to the Qur'an 6:38, it states: "There is not an animal (that lives) on the earth, nor a being that flies on its wings, but (forms part of) communities like you. Nothing have we omitted from the book, and they (all) shall be gathered to their Lord in the end."

This verse affords one a panoramic view of other communities, other than human communities, to be observed for guidance. So, when one observes nature, one will find that:

- Different birds form different communities
- Different tigers form different communities
- Different lions form different communities
- Different bison form different communities
- Different dolphins form different communities
- Different sharks form different communities
- Different whales form different communities,
- Different squirrels form different communities
- Different elephants form different communities
- Different snakes form different communities
- Different cows form different communities
- Different monkeys form different communities
- Different zebras form different communities.

And so with every other animal on the earth or being that flies on its wings, communities are formed, both individual and social, like human communities.

So, when one observes the care and nurturing that animals impart to their infants or young ones, one will find that they "**transfer**" to them the same skills that they possess. Here is a clue for those who are prehensile: truly, one has to be vigilant and circumspect in what one transfers to others. Coincidentally, this also suggests that children are capable of imbibing Allah's message at a very early stage of their lives. One just has to trust Allah.

Qur'an 31:16

“O my son!" (said Luqman), "If there be (but) the weight of a mustard-seed and It were (hidden) in a rock, Or (anywhere) in the heavens or On earth, Allah will bring if Forth: for Allah is subtle and Aware.”

When one refrains from following the guidance of Allah, one denies oneself the possibility for enlightenment! It's only Allah who can bring forth the hidden things, wherever they may be. The verb used for the word "bring" is imperfect, third-person, masculine singular in the accusative state. The imperfect tense denotes an incomplete action; it includes both present and future tenses. So, Allah is going to be bringing things forth now and in the future.

Qur'an 31:17

"O my son establish Regular prayer, enjoin what is Just, and forbid what is wrong: And bear with patience constancy Whatever betide thee; for this Is firmness (of purpose) In (the conduct of) affairs."

This is the formula that prevents transgression and maintains balance in one's life. This formula is not a partner of palliation (to relieve without curing), but it eradicates—moral, mental, intellectual, and spiritual insolvencies.

Qur'an 31:18

"And swell not thy cheek (For pride) at men. Nor walk in insolence Through the earth: For Allah loveth not Any arrogant boaster."

These are character altering behaviors that should without doubt be passed over for better orientations.

Qur'an 31:19

"Be moderate in your pace. And lower your voice, for the ugliest of all voices is certainly the braying of donkeys."

These basic principles are commonly shared by all members of Human- kind alike and need to be restored in all influential places that has a voice to make a difference.

MESSAGE FROM THE AUTHOR

It has not been, nor was it, my intention to present a tafsir (explanation, exposition, elucidation, or interpretation) to the preceding verses of the Qur'an. The Qur'an stands clear on its own merits! These are just social comments to address social needs for those who are socially receptive.

Shakir Maris Abdullah

PART THREE

During the preparation of this book, three questions were presented to me for consideration, which I will address as paramount and tantamount to the theme of this book.

QUESTION

In 31:12, the translated word Luqman used is "Allah." Is the word, in fact, Allah or God? If it is Allah, Allah is an Arabic word (other languages have other words to indicate Allah). Where did people live who spoke Arabic?

ANSWER

Etymologically, Allah is probably a contraction of the Arabic *al-ilah,* "the god." The origin of the name can be traced to the earliest Semitic writings in which the word for god was *IL* or *EL,* the latter being an Old Testament synonym for Yahweh. Allah is the standard Arabic word for God, used by Arab Christians as well as by Muslims.

Arabic is one of the world's most widely used languages. It is the official language of many Arab nations in the Middle East and Northern Africa, including Egypt, Iraq, Jordan, Lebanon, Saudi Arabia, and Syria.

No one knows when Arabic originally developed, but the people of the Arabian Peninsula were the first to use it. During the A.D. 600s, Islam spread throughout Southwest Asia and Northern Africa, and the Arabic language was introduced in these areas.

QUESTION

In 31:16, there is a word translated as "mustard-seed." Does the word in the Arabic text really mean mustard-seed, and if so, are mustard plants generic to any particular area or continent (this word is also used in the Bible)?

ANSWER

Mustard is any of several herbs of the genus *Brassica* or the condiment made from their pungent seeds. Mustard leaves are used as greens or potherbs. Both white (or yellow) mustard (*Brassica hirta*) and black (or brown) mustard (*Brassica nigra*) originated in the Mediterranean region or Western Temperate Asia and have been cultivated for at least 2,000 years. Today, they are found throughout most of the temperate regions of the world. Mustard plants are mentioned frequently in Greek and Roman writings and in the Bible; in the New Testament, the tiny seed is a symbol of faith. Mustard seed was used medicinally by Hippocrates.

QUESTION

In 31:17, the translated word is "prayer." What is the word in the Arabic text, and since this word indicates a particular criteria, in what area in the world was this criteria evident in their form of prayer?

ANSWER

Salat is the daily ritual prayer enjoined upon all Muslims as one of the five Pillars of Islam: *Salat al-fajr* (dawn), *Az-zuhr* (midday), *al-asr* (afternoon), *al-maghrib* (sunset), and *al-isha* (evening). Under special circumstances such as illness, a journey, or war, a modification or limited postponement of these salats is allowed. Though individual performance of salat is permissible, collective worship in the mosque has special merit. With their faces turned in the direction of the Ka'bah in Mecca, the worshippers align themselves in parallel rows behind the imam, or prayer leader, who directs them as they execute the rak'ahs (physical postures coupled with Qur'anic recitations).

SUMMARY

I assume these questions were posed to determine whether or not there existed a hermetic kinship between Luqman and the Arabs. However, this postulation—that there exists or may exist a birth connection between Luqman and the Arabs—is not categorically sound and does not establish Luqman as a hereditary member of the Arab dynasty for several reasons.

First, it has been verified and settled that Luqman's origin was of African descent. Consult part one of this book.

Second, it's probable that Luqman made an excursion from Africa to (or somewhere around) the Arabian Peninsula and cohabited and habituated to the Arabic language among Arabic-speaking people. Further, Arabic was not introduced into northern Africa until around A.D. 600, well after Luqman's wisdom had been recorded among the Arabs as memorable and legendary. Moreover, Luqman's notability as a sage amidst the Arabs was well in advance of Muhammad's inculcation or teaching of Al-Islam, which indicates that Luqman journeyed or migrated to that region prior to the advent of Islam in Makkah or Africa.

Third, just because Luqman's devotions are associated with beliefs and rituals that emanated from Arabian localities does not in any way provide a birth link between one or the other of these sentients. Upon arriving in a different geographical and social climate, one would have to adapt to its offerings or be an outcast to its interactions. Additionally, the significance of the mustard seed or plant should be expounded here. Even though the mustard has been referred to as a symbol of faith in the Bible, it still had to be a prevalent or widely existing seed in that region in order to draw the message or conclusion that the saying intended to teach in the Bible.

Likewise, the same application applies to Luqman's depiction of the mustard seed. To put it another way, if a comparison is drawn between two objects and one of those objects is unobservable or unavailable to provide contrasting distinctions, the lesson or message would be lost or meaningless! Therefore, the mustard seed had to be endemic to Luqman's surroundings for observation, in order for the full effect of his teaching about the mustard seed to be realized or galvanizing.

And finally, Luqman, unlike Abraham, Jacob, Ismail, Isaac, and Muhammad—who were divinely instructed through inspiration and scriptures to worship One God, or, in the case of Jacob, Ismail, and Isaac, to worship the God of their fathers—had no such procedural history to adhere to as a format. Nor did Luqman instruct his son to follow any formal genealogy.

Nevertheless, Luqman's life was in harmony with the

teachings of the prophets. He urged his son to embrace this same path, which he had, in fact, adopted from the excellent paradigm of the prophets. Indeed, this admonition employed to Luqman's son would ensure the parallelism of the prophets' teachings in his son's life while simultaneously omitting the reference to those whom Luqman received the teachings from, yet promoting and advocating the one who made the teachings available and possible—(Allah)! There is no god but Allah! There is always room for further human growth.

Every tribe, nation, or people, past and present, have a place in the Qur'an, including individuals. For Africans (of all residents, states, and countries), because of slave conditioning through the slave-consciousness movement, "slaves be obedient to your masters," were reoriented with all kinds of self-destructive behaviors that this work has come to reclaim to mental normalcy. Once the problem is located, the Qur'an will provide the solution. It is a panacea if given the chance to speak. The above scenario with Luqman and his son is equivalent to the Africans', of all residents, states, and countries, dilemma—not the Arabs' dilemma.

Qur'an 39:41

"Surely, We have revealed to you the Book ˹O Prophet˺ with the truth for humanity. So whoever chooses to be guided, it is for their own good. And whoever chooses to stray, it is only to their own loss. You are not a keeper over them."

This preview of Luqman's distinctiveness should erase any attempt to presuppose that he was other than African with a message to his inherit successors.

CONCLUSION

If these divine and experimentally proved virtues illustrated and demonstrated in Luqman's dialogue could be implanted into the minds and hearts and subsequently released through actions by all contemporary Africans (of all states, residents, and countries), excluding those who already possess these virtues, their lives would greatly improve. "Children deprived of such virtues as mentioned in Luqman's discourse tend to become morally, socially, and mentally defective."

One of the most explosive and prolific facts to attest to this defectiveness is the number of incarcerated Africans (of all states, residents, and countries) confined in prisons and jails throughout the United States. While many are released as being wrongfully convicted and many are detained as guilty as charged, this does not in any way reflect defectiveness. "Defectiveness lies in the inability to make intelligent mental and moral selections, which would ultimately benefit their choices or land them in undesirable and regrettable situations and places." Their selection-making process contains an element of freedom but also a risk of failure that, if not properly managed or carefully exercised, will result in mental and moral delinquency.

Many sociological studies show that the bulk of juvenile delinquents are recruited from children who, in their early life, did not have the necessary minimum education of virtues.

Deficiency of "the vitamins of virtues" is also responsible for many mental disorders. Virtues are a very powerful antidote against criminal and morbid tendencies. However, if these facts are continuously disregarded, society will continue to decline mentally and morally, both the poor and the educated. The poor because they are struggling without correct mental and moral leadership, and the educated because they are applying wrong methods to solve these crises, which indicates their lack of "human sentiments."

Every narrative that the Qur'an offers is for the purpose of solving specific problems and difficulties. Even so, in their diverse corrections, all these narratives lead to the same "goal"—the unification of God and living a righteous life! Every community, race, nation, and people has a distinct liability, and for the Africans (of all states, residents, and countries), that distinct liability is the breakdown of the father and son matrix, as photographed in Luqman's picture.

BIBLIOGRAPHY

- The Meaning Of The Qur'an. By: Abul A'la Maududi
- The Noble Qur'an. By: Allama Shabbir Ahmad Usmani
- The Qur'an. By: T.B. Irving
- The Glorious Qur'an. By: Mohammed Marmaduke Pickthall
- The Holy Qur'an. By: Ayatullah Agla H.M.M. Pooya Yazid S.V. Mir Ahmed Ali
- The Holy Qur'an. By: Maulana Muhammad Ali
- The Holy Qur'an. By: Abdullah Yusuf Ali
- Vocabulary Of The Holy Qur'an. By: Dr. Abdullah Abbas Nadwi
- Tafsir Ibn Kathir. By: Ibn Kathir
- Tafsir At-Tabari. By: At-Tabari
- Dictionary Of The Holy Qur'an. By: "Abdul Mannan "Omar

BIBLIOGRAPHY

EPILOGUE I

My preceptor, Imam K. Awwal Abdur Raheem, had taught me concerning the truth: to seek it, to find it, and to live it. However, these particulars can only be amply fulfilled where coexisting stipulations permit the establishment of such truth. Otherwise, the experience will be tantalizing and overbearing.

An aware teacher would always advise his or her apprentice to seek the truth and reality according to their possession of feasibility. This has been a lesson taught, learned, and effected through this feasible channel to expose the Luqman saga. Imam K. Awwal Abdur Raheem was the first Muslim prison chaplain, now retired, to be employed in the state of Massachusetts for over 20 years.

I sincerely dedicate this book in part to him, that he may know his services were not without response and awakening, given the conditions of my physical limitations. However, I am solely responsible for the contents of this book, and I may be the sole beneficiary of any obloquy and a gregarious extrovert to any societal advancement.

I believe I have presented a fair and accurate assessment of that truth. I was led to seek, to find, and to live within the contents unearthed in this book. Africans have always sought some concrete connection to link them with their predecessors, to substantiate that they were human like other people and came from civilized backgrounds. And though archaeological excavations attested to their humanity, advanced conventions, and civilization, they were still looked upon as less than other human beings. These conditions have somewhat improved in these modern days of information. But this falsehood had mainly continued to circulate because their true history had been misplaced or lost altogether, and they were subjected to all kinds of menial occupations, like Moses' people had endured and experienced under Pharaoh's tyranny.

The truth that has been excavated now is what was needed to challenge that shame and absurdity Africans (of all residents, states, and countries) had been subjected to in the past and present!

Africans' (of all residents, states, and countries) history

has not been buried in the ground where some archaeologists have sought.

Qur'an 11:120 states:

"All that we relate to thee of the messengers, with it we make firm thy heart: in them there cometh to thee the Truth as well as an exhortation and a message of remembrance to those who believe."

The narratives of the messengers in the Qur'an contain the following elements at all times:

1. They teach the highest spiritual Truth.
2. They give advice, direction, and warning as to how we should govern our lives.
3. They awaken our conscience and remind us of the working of Allah's (God's) Law in human affairs.

Therefore, African history has been contained in sacred scripture (the Qur'an), which most seekers have inadvertently overlooked repeatedly. However, once divine truth is lost, the excavation of past relics is employed to find the truth. The message in this book is the lost heirloom of the global African people's psyche.

As a member of the global African populace with a sordid past as equal to or heftier than that of Malcolm X, I have sought, as Malcolm sought. First, to gain education to address my own deficiencies, and secondly, to make a contribution to society in a significant way while avoiding being categorized as a pariah. It would be a shame, disgrace, and utter loss for me to reside under the roof of Norfolk Colony, where Malcolm X received his alma mater, and not make any change, any progress, or any social contribution to the legacy he has left here at Norfolk Colony. I would be completely crushed and irate because all my roaming at Norfolk would have been frolic.

I inscribe the remaining part of this book to Malcolm for his passion and stamina to awaken the human conscience in a resilient way. I adopt and endorse that aspiration under the aegis of The Holy Qur'an. Luqman's hallmark was his gratitude to the wisdom of Allah, which is always better than worldly or man-made guidance.

EPILOGUE II

This is not an autobiography, only protruding details relative to my current and immediate experience that should be included as germane to the other parts of this book.

It's really ironic that I grew up without a father figure in my life. Though my father's name is actually "Prophet," he played no leadership role in my life. I sometimes wonder, "What intentions did his parents have for his future?" The contemplation of this reverie reminded me of a situation I read in the Holy Qur'an.

Mary, the mother of Jesus, whose mother, Hannah (in Latin, Anna, and in English, Anne), had expected during her pregnancy to have a child that she could dedicate and devote totally to the service of God.

However, when she delivered the neonate, it was a female

child instead of a male child. The female child could not be devoted to Temple service under the Mosaic law, as she had intended. This temporarily foreclosed her special purposes for the child. But little did she expect that her daughter, Mary, would be the mother of Jesus, the savior of his people, and the fulfiller of Mary's mother's foreboded plans.

So, with a name such as "Prophet," I can only imagine what high expectations his parents had for his future career, which may really manifest itself through his child and not through his parents' plan, as in the case of Mary's mother, Hannah.

It is also ironic that my mother always favored me above her other three children. For whatever reason, she never revealed it to me. Nevertheless, what is becoming clear to me now that I have contact with divine influence (the Qur'an) in my life is that I've been taught some things that, perhaps, I need to use to help others if they are corrigible. This book is the first step to a life of change.

www.ingramcontent.com/pod-product-compliance
Lightning Source LLC
LaVergne TN
LVHW050343160826
845677LV00014B/3766

* 9 7 9 8 8 9 6 9 1 0 9 5 4 *